Barry Cottrell is an artist, writer and visionary. Born in Bristol, England in 1953, he studied psychology and philosophy at Oxford University and art at the Ruskin School of Drawing and Fine Art. As an artist-printmaker, he works mainly with a burin on copper, wood or lino to produce 'poetry of the driven line.' As a researcher, he has explored and written about human consciousness and the recovery of primal mind.

Other books by Barry Cottrell:

The Way Beyond The Shaman:
Birthing A New Earth Consciousness
O Books/Moon Books, 2008

Entering Earth's Time:
A Pleiadian Perspective for Planetary Awakening
independently published, 2019

Sounding Eternity
BARRY COTTRELL

*Shamanic Incantations and the
Poetics of Sonic Power*

driven*L*ine

First published as *The Black River Trilogy* in Sofia, Bulgaria by Lessedra Contemporary Art Projects in 2018. www.lessedra.com

First published as *Sounding Eternity* in 2021 by drivenLine. www.drivenline.uk/soundingeternity

Text © Barry Cottrell 2021
Illustrations © Barry Cottrell 2021
The right of Barry Cottrell to be identified as the author of this work has been asserted by him in accordance with the Copyright, Designs and Patents Act, 1988.

ISBN 978-1-7-7399205-0-0

All rights reserved. No part of this publication may be reproduced, stored in or introduced into a retrieval system, or transmitted in any form, or by any means (electronic, mechanical, photo-copying, recording or otherwise) without the prior written permission of the copyright holder.

drivenLine, The Clock House, Widford, Burford
OX18 4DU

Cover design and illustration by the author, showing detail of the engraving, *Sonetto*

CONTENTS

Acknowledgements	vi
Preface	viii
The Black River Trilogy	1
Down the Black River	2
Cycle of Low	8
Court of the High Minute	16
Afterword	27
References	40
Artist's statement	43

LIST OF ILLUSTRATIONS

dhāranī, 2018, burin engraving on copper, 10 x 10cm	vii
The Prayer, 2002, burin engraving on copper, 20 x 15cm	xvii
polka dot madonna, 2020, burin engraving on copper, 10 x 10cm	26
Sonetto, 2013, burin engraving on copper, 12 x 7.5cm	42
sounding (detail), 2000, linocut, 8 x 7.5cm	45

ACKNOWLEDGEMENTS

With thanks to Georgi Kolev for his special presentation of The Black River Trilogy at the exhibition of Lessedra Mini Print 2018 in Sofia, Bulgaria, and for printing and publishing the trilogy in the exhibition catalogue.

Also deep gratitude to artist-printmaker Eva Choung-Fux, first prize winner of Lessedra Mini Print Annual 2017, and jury member in 2018, for giving her recital from The Black River Trilogy at the opening of Lessedra Mini Print 2018 in June 2018, and for her dedication in the exhibition catalogue, printed on the back cover of this book.

dhāraṇī, 2018, burin engraving on copper

PREFACE

While the words in this book are presented as poems, they originated as sound, vocalisations and ritual utterances, made during a shamanic state of consciousness.

Shamanism is the world's most ancient surviving technique for accessing worlds beyond everyday physical reality. It was known to the whole of archaic humanity and was being practiced by our Paleolithic ancestors during the last ice age, at least thirty thousand years ago, in the caves of southern France and northern Spain.

The practices of the shaman were immortalised in the title of historian Mircea Eliade's classic text, *Shamanism: Archaic techniques of ecstasy*.[1] While ecstasy is normally thought of as an experience of spiritual exaltation, rapture or bliss, when applied to shamanism it refers specifically to their 'magical flight'–the altered state of consciousness which the shaman enters in order to cross over the threshold between worlds and to 'journey' through the metaphysical domain. In this timeless state the wisdom of the shamanic universe can be tapped, like the source of a spring high up on a mountain.

The vehicle for this magical flight is usually monotonous drumming, although in some cultures other means are used to induce an altered state of consciousness. Especially important in Central and South America is the use of magical plants to release the soul from the body to embark upon the shamanic journey. For example, the Huichols of Mexico ingest *hikuri*, the hallucinogenic cactus peyote, while the Tukanoan peoples of the northwest Amazon drink the bitter *ayahuasca*, the 'vine of the soul,' in order to confer with the spirits of the forest. The Yanomami of the Venezuelan Amazon inhale *ebena*, the 'semen of the sun,' which completely dissolves the shaman's experience of ordinary reality.

Despite this wide use of hallucinatory drugs by South American shamans, riding the sound of the drum is the most universal, and possibly the most archaic method–especially in the Northern Hemisphere–used by shamans for entering other realities. The use of sound has always been central to the rituals and ceremonies of tribal peoples. But the drum is distinguished from all the other instruments that produce sound, including the voice, by the fact that it propels the shaman out of the body and off onto the shamanic journey. It is truly a vehicle, a means of transport, and is often called a 'horse.' It was the shamanic technique used to produce the utterances and incantations of *The Black River Trilogy*.

Having arrived in the timeless zone—the "eternity"–of the shamanic universe, it became possible to "communicate without fear through the keyhole of eternity" and articulate coherent visions from the extraordinary perspective of this realm. There is the sense that the ritual of the shamanic journey somehow re-establishes a primordial unity with the cosmos. A deep inhalation of the 'etheric' atmosphere marks the beginning of the utterances: words emerge very slowly at first as densely cryptic sounds, as strings of often seemingly nonsensical phonemes, which then coalesce into strangely coherent hyper-meaningful texts. The words of the incantations are recorded and later transcribed as narrative verse.

Utterances of this kind have precedents in their mode of production: shamans throughout history and prehistory have been known to utter trance-induced, seemingly nonsense 'words of power,' often as part of a healing ritual or ceremony. Healing energy is conveyed through the power of sound, bypassing the conventional meaning of words.

In medieval China, Buddhist monks of the Tang dynasty would utter *dhāranī*, incantations which would also convey the power to heal or protect, despite being at times totally incomprehensible. Historian of religion, Paul Copp observes: "…the Incantation's impenetrability is a function not of the empty meaninglessness of its phrases but of the supramundane intensity of their fullness and profundity."[2] For premodern Chinese monks these rites of consecration–the *dhāraṇī*–were not only the sounds uttered through their mouths; they could also be expressed as profoundly meaningful liturgical texts, inscribed on paper as woodcut prints, or even carved in stone.

In his essay on Dante, T.S. Eliot says that the task of the poet is to make people comprehend the incomprehensible and that genuine poetry can communicate before it is understood: "…in good allegory, like Dante's, it is not necessary to understand the meaning first to enjoy the poetry." He goes on to say that "it is our enjoyment of the poetry that makes us want to understand the meaning."[3]

As sacramental narrative verse, the poems in *The Black River Trilogy* address the contemporary human condition with an important message: in the words of the Greek Orthodox prelate, John

Zizioulas, Metropolitan bishop of Pergamon:

"In our Western culture we did everything to de-sacralise life, to fill our societies with legislators, moralists and thinkers, and undermined the fact that the human being is also, or rather primarily, a liturgical being, faced from the moment of birth with a world that he or she must treat either as a sacred gift or as raw material for exploitation and use."[4]

The utterances and sounds which gave rise to this book come from a level of awareness and intelligence beyond the physical yet possessing a sensitivity and deep concern for our human vulnerability when we are faced with the choices and challenges of incarnate freewill. In his song "Highlands" from the album *Time Out Of Mind*, legendary singer-songwriter Bob Dylan expresses this human predicament: "Well I'm lost somewhere, I must have made a few bad turns."

The poems in this book are invocations and, at times, cryptic exhortations: they ask us to consider how the Western world has strayed into the dead-end of secular materialism; yet they also present a mystical vision of redemption. In the stillness of a mind out of time the wisdom of the shamanic universe is tapped, like the source of a spring high up on a mountain, offering a balm for the soul.

The three poems in this trilogy emerged in 1993 at a time when I was deeply engaged in the exploration of the shamanic universe. The purpose of my quest in these three inner journeys was to explore the relationship between power and empowerment in the last decade of the 20th century–to examine the way in which the abuse of power had corrupted our civilization and devastated the earth. Yet the trilogy also presents a utopian vision in which new ways of living and more mature ways of being can transform our relationships and help turn the planet into a more wholesome and benign place as our common home.

Today the abuse of power and the need for true empowerment of all people has intensified onto a new apocalyptic level. *The Black River Trilogy* was—and still is—an allegory of our times, a mystical vision of redemption and the rebirth of sacramental consciousness.

Barry Cottrell July 2021

The Prayer, 2002, burin engraving on copper

"Eternity is in love with the productions of time." *–William Blake*

"So we stood, alive in the river of light, Among the creatures of light, creatures of light."*–Ted Hughes*

"In the beginning, there was no beginning. Life on Earth is a particle of Eternity perceived strangely through the lens of passing time." *–Barry Cottrell*

THE BLACK RIVER TRILOGY

Down The Black River

Keep down the strident call
for empathy
with tentative, fleeting gestures.
Humble the canopy
which stretches up to laden skies—
peak of dynasty
yet falling through the crater.

Liberation through simple,
undisguised poetic climate
of re-enchanted loam,
and ether-sifted,
salient features
dawn in mists
from future conquests
where no blood is spilled,
no creature dies.

Yet up the soaked Poor fly
in seed-beds of past domains.
Into each and every highway
go the coloration
and perspicacity
of no ending story–
hinted tales of Pagan times
which led to raunching Lent.

Systematic transitions
keep the time
and keep the trade
of glorifying salesmen
handy as can be
to re-embrace the loaded dice
and hurl them through the sky
to strike a chord
of merciful delinquency
through which the story
disembowels its hora,
like the times which we can see

are only rubbing,
ribbed hallucinations.
And, each time,
we taste the chorus-saving sleep
of drone and drone
and ode for long-suffering
separate age.

Aeon upon endless rage
and drifting tundra tasks
have accomplished
all they needed
of their own complacent
taking of the Torch
which drifted down
the Black River's current
to the deep, deep, deep Blue Sea
and sank until it shone
from yonder depth
and lit the Pearl of Wisdom

which we sought
but yet could not place.

So when that Fish embodied
those lit embers of our Grace
and opened wide its mouth
so we could see our show
reflected in the gill
which breathed no air
and we could see no pair of eyes
to gleam through that dream-
ridden escapade,
our moment came
and still our moment comes
when drums the day along
and trance disguises lit-up night
for day
and we continue drifting on
until the seeds complete
the bursting rupture
of our clefted symbols;

and encompassed harvest
is now ripe
for cascading
these simple sliding pips
to reap the sewing.

Owing more than we can tell
in Time, yet once removed
is open up for question:
how can Thy Name be Hallowed
when the same shows
in each and every spark
of Light as Thy am I
and Ye are Me?
And sealing the rift
between these ancient adversaries,
hoping for a new constitution.

To each rendered "Hail" many times
and calling back the river
from its source to the sea;

and in that relocation,
I see this simple equation,
and it is simple:
safe places,
havens in the wake of races;
pale complexions pour
from the sections
which are shocked,
fatal attraction,
sealing the sign of the times
with a cross.

Playing out,
raying out:
signify your stridence.
Come,
come by.

Cycle of Low

Moving down

with complete, hallowed Radiance
to stumbling grace
and pillars simply cast down,
the sorrow hampering,
to culminate in trembling tone
of the last time
when we all came here
into the hell-bent race
to reach out for a time
when all is as Imagined
as can be.

Using our Lady,
Lady of the Lake,
she says:
"Ask, each time
you want to come

into this place;
because, you see,
it is not so easy
just to come
and your wrenching complications
drastically reduce
the size of the port-hole."

And when *they* came
and saw the state of the traces
and laden ropes
(which stretched and frayed
until the weight became
so unsupportable
that "uff," "uff,"
up from the Depths
the Serpent came
from dream-laced depths
of the Sea
to support the rocking canopy,

the raft at sea,
and "Hallowed Be
our entry to a brighter future"),
a sting in the tail
was so maidenly traded
for the colour of our eyes
when they see
what they no longer need.

But the lines go drifting
down the current,
catching all that come
before the net,
its weight drags down
the Beautiful Boat
in which we were trawling
for our Sakes.
The Cargo sank
and all were consigned
to the place of their prey.

And in a shaft of light
which penetrated
the Blazing Blackness
of the devouring Ocean,
I saw an alien, temperamental estate,
which, rubbering around
our local endeavours,
trips the switch
and shoots down
all attempts to redeem.

Yet in the sane, Sounding-Place
where joins the Chorus
to the supplicating streams,
we continue
to dialogue,
to free those emblems
which became so encrusted
in the grain-soaked residue.

Too soon the rules will be changing;
too soon the shock will be raging
and ravens 'crark'
and dog in midnight bark,
howling the hollow silence,
as we see the aeons
of endless populating
give out to that graceful,
that sensational,
Last Call to remember,
Last Call to relocate.

And the Maiden takes her slip
and shifts to a new position,
willing the consummation,
willing the Retro-raider on
from pulsing grasp
to dance with Her
and sweat-drip the rhythm,
consummating all those unspoken,

sleepless dreams
as she drifts towards
his stunned Awakening.

In each they seek
the barely-consecrated
naked truth.

But sorrow is the season
before the Beam,
the reaching down to caskets
in deep and thick, unbreathing cavern
where the fingertips pick pearls
which gleam in black
and which are daylight
encapsulating
tree-dripped dew
of maiden secrets.

And we saw it all
before we came
and forgot the purpose
of our naming,
itemising,
playing.

"So see where you are now:
silently protect your Mayline."

I was born in a place
which was no repast:
It was the sighing Frome.
The sighing Frome
with licking banks
and oh, so tasty plastic trash,
plantations of employing tasks.

And so long as the Afterlife comes in,
there's no time to see the Sun.

Cycle of Low:
"I must see the fruit
before I plant the seed.
I have no faith nor vision,
no long, low-wave frequency,
no sound to echo back the outcome."
And the in-growing cables
electrify those traders
as they please themselves
and wrench the Carbon
from the Fire.

"We shall lead a way and Radiate–
sickness will away"–
and smile, smile, smile,
as the Rock of Ageless roasting
rakes the floor of the forest.
My sign is the Sign
of the Po-faced, Porky,
Palladium Master.

Court of the High Minute

Silent rights seek a voice
that intones release.
And the spent invitation hardens
into a brief carve-up
of the scene.

And in that time
the melody turned to sonic boom,
each trader leading the way
in the tide of estranged cases
to the Court of the High Minute,
as the last rays of hope
were setting in the fields
beyond the din
of petulant persuasion
to elope with the Silver Service

before the mark on the table-top
was noticed.
And the thief in the night
was petrified by daylight.

The travesty of the Paler Minstrels:
they danced their way
along the street
and kept their feet
which touched the ground
on hardened stone.

But they danced down the root
and grew to be
the Ponderous Prelate,
aye, they lost their feet
and lost the movement
in their knee,

sitting in judgement,
grasping all within their reach,
unable to move
or shift their feet;
disempowered,
prosaic mongering,
no poetic licence
nor breathing
simply soft.

Green acres,
lake and foliage
contain a power to renew.

But in the sip,
sweet-tasting tipple of managers
with rosin-rubbed,
vibrating strings

and humble, pectoral pleadings,
let's sign the times
with a kiss…

So infinitely tempted am I
to repatriate myself
into a solar system
where the Moon has shone
its last reflection
and been re-embedded
into cordless reign
of the whole
of the paved Universe.

Stepping back,
I reach for the augury
and re-erase the space
beneath the traded template.

The One which came before
is now replacing
the One which came after,
and we have been soaking up
the residue
to spew forth
a spate of wrath,
rocking lessons
for ourselves
and "for our children,
and our childrens' children,
and their children,
and their childrens' children,"
seeking,
loaded,
playing,
pleading:

"Simply after the sacred,
simply after the ladenless,
simply after the space filled in
the solar plexus,
full to breathing free,
away, away, away."

And so we took our leave
of the steaming archipelago,
where our Host forgot to enter
our names into the guest-book.
We left and tried to scratch
the emblematic mark
in stone,
in tree,
in sky,
in sea,
until we saw our so-called selves

in every place,
until we ruined
each displaced process
of Becoming–
as we always *really* knew we could.

And we wandered down
through all those places,
sat down and scratched our names
in radiant hand–
wasted, wasted, wasted–
yet knowing all in vain
until we turned around
and saw that our Host had joked
and entered all we knew
so Each was Everyone
come to proclaim
their heavenly status.

But the time came
when no-one saw the steam
coming from a crack in the wall;
and some time ago
the stench of putrefaction
led to embalming
the previous summer's
left-over debris.

I am rooting
for a simple solution.
We can tell the rate
of the cumulative effects:
it's accelerating to a point
where all is caught up
in the Slip-Stream.
And extraneous complaints
will be sifted and sorted

into what can be of use
and what cannot.

I am looking at those fields
where nothing can be seen
by eyes which have been spiked
by tried-and-tested–
failed–
pursed lips
and morgue-enhanced rituals
which re-animate
the miscreated.

The odour wafts across at last
and, looking down into the pool,
all is residual–
posthumous price
for casting the line

which has found
a harvest of seed-pods.

The aid we sought
cannot be grasped or forced—
it slips through gritted fingers
and, elusive,
falls between the cells
which spark
and, uttering,
complies with the Order
which is wider than our heart,
beyond, around,
and closer than can be known.

polka dot madonna, 2020, burin engraving on copper

AFTERWORD

This essay was originally written in May 1997 when I had already uttered the incantations of *The Black River Trilogy* (in the summer of 1993) and the shamanic path had become well-established as a central quest in my life. In *The Marriage of Heaven and Hell*, William Blake famously wrote: "Eternity is in love with the productions of time" and this book is an expression of that love, waiting almost thirty years to be produced after the sounds that created it were uttered.

Underlying the utterances which produced these poems was the shamanic dissolution and reshaping of self. This essay explores the further potential for releasing the Western psyche from solitary confinement in the monotheistic prison of the self, and from the tyranny of extreme self-consciousness.

"It is not impossible to imagine a time, perhaps beyond our known historical world, when people would use words and concepts without the fixedness of meaning with which we use them today; a time when meaning would arise almost organically from the sounds of words during their utterance and from the relationships between those sounds; a time when words themselves were less abstract, less prone to become set in cement.

The mark of this ancient–or future–consciousness would be a dynamically perceptual process of richly interrelating imagery. The emphasis would be on the so-called 'right-brain' activity in a culture which had become predominantly intuitive. Instinct would play an equal if not greater part in daily life than intellect. If words were used, their meanings would be adopted only for as long as they were needed and would then be shelved. Today the words of certain kinds of music and poetry may still hint at this fluidity and transience of meaning.

A poem can be a universe unto itself, holding together perceptions and images in a relationship which lasts as long as the time it takes to utter the sounds within it. At the end of the poem we are left with the resonance created during the utterance of those sounds. It is this resonance, this rhythmical expansion of energy which has the capacity to loosen the fixedness of meaning and free us from the gravitational pull of literalness, to which modern consciousness has become so very committed.

Words and their meanings today, instead of being ephemeral, expressing momentary perceptions, passing insights and images, have become so fixed and literal that anything we say may be 'taken down' and 'used against us.' Permanent, indelible, they become tools for conflict and misunderstanding. The words 'I,' for example, or 'you' in the singular, express the concept of a single, isolated self which we generally believe to be the ultimate essence of who we are as individuals. This concept has become so deeply ingrained in Western culture that most of us believe, as the great psychologist James Hillman has pointed out, that we have a "heroic immovable centre" to our being, the solitary, unpopulated core that remains to sustain us "when all else has gone."[5]

We live under the tyranny of this concept. For in order to maintain the existence and continuity of this self, along with its individuality and separateness, we are committed to the perpetual stress of ongoing self-conscious reflection. This monumental task can only be achieved and sustained by denying the validity of other more expansive and symbolic forms of cognition beyond our fixation on self-consciousness. For example, French scholar Lucien Lévy-Bruhl's *'participation mystique'* is a highly valued aspect of sacred ritual among tribal communities which have retained their shamanic roots. The shaman will lose self-consciousness in order to merge with his or her power animal, or 'ally,' and undertake a healing ritual. This un-self-consciousness, when combined with relaxed attention, allows for real cognition or 'knowing.' It is the means *par excellence* for entering into and truly understanding the 'interior' or soul of the world around us.

Medical anthropologist David Napier believes that this conflation of self and other is "a natural state to which we return at every moment not controlled by culturally prescribed, self-conscious reflection."[6] However, not to be self-conscious in our society is taboo–the sign of a regressive, infantile or 'primitive' mentality. Sigmund Freud contributed to this cultural paranoia about conflating self and other by advising that we should succeed in overcoming the "animistic primary processes" in the natural course of personal growth.

In other words, we should overcome the childlike, natural tendency to identify with things–to experience the world around us as alive, animated, and imbued with spirit. We are taught to deny that anything beyond the solitary human self has soul. We are taught especially to suppress the need to commune with spirits in other life-forms around us, such as trees, sky, the winds, or animals.

Our society has come to value self-conscious reflection above all other modes of psychic experience and to denigrate any form of cognition not characterised by self-consciousness—even simple 'day-dreaming.' As Napier says, "…a good person, a better person, is one who maintains the capacity for self-conscious reflection."[7]

Clearly this solitary confinement of the 'self,' sustained by the ongoing effort of acute self-consciousness, has been an important and necessary step in the evolution of our peculiarly Western consciousness. Perhaps we have needed this intense fixation of awareness in order to incarnate more deeply into the material world. Perhaps one day we will move beyond the need for this extreme focussed egocentrism. However, both individually and collectively, it has become a 'one-party' state of the self, very much based on the fear of losing that experience of self. And because there is only one self to lose, the fear is total and overwhelming, with the alternative to loss of self being nothing and oblivion.

The fear of losing this self is usually expressed through devaluing or denigrating 'otherness,' things which may seem strange or alien. As Napier points out, "…the more we devalue any sort of experience that is not self-reflective or narcissistic, the less capable we are of appreciating any sort of value in the alien."[8] The alien might be something as simple as the un-self-conscious experience of trees 'talking' or hills 'singing' to us, or communing with the spirit of a bee; these are experiences which society mocks and dismisses, labelling as 'eccentric' if not 'psychotic' those who have them.

In order to break out of the monotheistic prison of this self, we need to find ways to re-imagine ourselves. We need to be able at times to shelve this fixed notion of the self as Hillman's "heroic immovable isolated centre…a single monad, an inner replica of a single God"[9] and adapt it, allowing it to become more expanded, flexible and fluid, inhabited by many spirits, many gods and goddesses. Hillman, for example, proposes "…a compound Self of several voices in several rooms…the focus or locus of visitations and semi-permanent residential inhabitants both dead and alive, both older than us and not yet born, both of this world and of other worlds–and interiorizations as well of the various communities to which we give allegiance in daily life."[10]

Re-imagining ourselves in this way allows us to 're-member' in the truest sense of the word. We become more aware of the many selves which need to converge on that point of consciousness which is who we are now. We are able to enter into and reconnect with all aspects of life around us, urban life, the natural world, other people, and respond to them, seeing them and ourselves as parts of the whole, as aspects of the collective dream to which we are all wedded.

Re-imagining ourselves allows us to recognise the consciousness within other forms of life and so to reconnect with the planet as a living, breathing, whole being. Expanding our awareness in this way into the larger, wider multitude of the self may loosen the tightness, easing the tensions which have arisen over centuries from limiting and fixing consciousness to the single physical frame, the body having become the prime symbol of the solitary self.

Re-imagining ourselves as 'the many' rather than being singularly frozen in stone—and in time—also allows a freer flow through the chapters of our lives. We may be whoever we need to be for the duration and purpose of whatever experience we are going through. As T.S. Eliot wrote in his poem *Little Gidding*: "I was still the same, Knowing myself yet being someone other."[11]

When we have finished with an experience, we may gently move on into the next episode with the emphasis shifting perhaps to another self, so that we become "someone other." We learn to let go gracefully when it is time to move on, knowing, as Hillman says, that "We are never alone; not in solitary confinement, not in meditative contemplation, not on the death bed. No towers and no walls can keep the spirits out."[12]

Letting in the spirits has resulted in this book. Its contents have come into being not only through a re-imagining of self, but also through a dissolution and reshaping of self, so that–like air or the breeze–the focus has become unfixed, more fluid and ether-like, breathing into the cracks between the worlds and passing through what the great British thinker, Owen Barfield, described as "the impenetrable fringe of that mysterious no-man's land which lies between words and their meanings."[13]

The words of these poems were utterances before being written down, their meanings carried by the resonance the sounds set up. The words dip to and fro often beyond intellectual apprehension. There is the hope here that, by being baffled somewhat, intellect may loosen its grip and allow us to roam more freely into the wider, many terrains of self so that it is no longer a question of 'Who are you?' but as Hillman suggests: 'Where are you? Where do you stop and start?'"[14]

References: Preface

1. Mircea Eliade, *Shamanism: Archaic techniques of ecstasy.* (London: Arkana, 1989).

2. Paul Copp, "Anointing Phrases and Narrative Power: A Tang Buddhist Poetics of Incantation." *History of Religions,* Vol. 52, No. 2, Narrative and Incantation in Chinese Buddhism (November 2012): 142-172.

3. T.S. Eliot, "What Dante Means to Me." *The Kenyon Review,* Vol. 14, No. 2, The Dante Number (Spring, 1952): 178-188.

4. John Zizioulas, Metropolitan bishop of Pergamon, "Proprietors or Priests of Creation?" *Keynote Address of the Fifth Symposium of Religion, Science, and the Environment* (June 2, 2003, Plenary Session 1).

References: Afterword

5, 9, 10, 12, 14. James Hillman, "Psychology, Self and Community," *Resurgence* 166, (July/August 1994): 18-21.

6, 7, 8. A. David Napier, "A Social Theory of the Person" in *Foreign Bodies: Performance, Art, and Symbolic Anthropology.* (Berkeley and Los Angeles: The University of California Press, 1992): 176-200.

11. T.S. Eliot, 'Little Gidding," in *Collected Poems 1909-1962 by T.S Eliot.* (London: Faber & Faber, 1974), 217.

13. Owen Barfield, *History in English Words.* (Edinburgh: Floris Books, 1967), 177.

Sonetto, 2013, burin engraving on copper

ARTIST'S STATEMENT

The steel tip of the burin, as it is driven through copper plate, gives rise to the elastic tension and beauty of the engraved line, and sets fire to the imagination.

I work mostly as an engraver and printmaker using a burin on copper plate, also burin on wood and lino. The burin is like a key unlocking the mythic realm of the imagination. I generally approach the engraving of a copper plate without preconceptions in order "to move into a zone of unintelligibility, the only place where the possibility of discovery lies, where the future is not at the outset already a thing of the past." (John Cage) As Deleuze and Guattari wrote in *A Thousand Plateaus* (1980): "We have no system, only lines and movements."

Conceptually, the ultimate purpose of all my artistic work and intellectual research is the 're-enchantment of the world' - seeking a reconnection with the 'primal' participatory mind. Making a mark or driving a line through resistant material is fundamentally a human act of incarnation – a physical inscription asserting presence and duration. Making marks and lines also has, I maintain, a profoundly liturgical aspect reflecting an essentially human need to connect and commune with realms of intelligence and experience which are not bounded by time and space.

*

sounding (detail), 2000, linocut

www.ingramcontent.com/pod-product-compliance
Lightning Source LLC
Chambersburg PA
CBHW071813160426
43209CB00003B/63